YEARNINGS:

A Memoir in Prose & Poetry

By William H. McCann, Jr.

Dad and me, October 1956, Lexington

(Mom the photographer)

Cover Photo: A Blurry Future, April 1962

Red always makes Mom stand out,
        as I stand beside her — in my dull
                but warm coat
I am proud owner of newly earned 'good' papers

Mom's gloved hand keeps me still.
        Though she smiles,
I wear a sad half-smile

A wide limestone handrail leads up to:
        "The Cove Schools"
A prophetic sign nearly too blurry to read

The road home leads
        through The Cove Schools

Dad is taking the picture: Making everyone look
        good as usual, out of the picture
and making things happen

Yet, before I can go home
        I must go up the steps,
Open the heavy Gothic door
        and go to work

The road home leads
        through The Cove Schools

Forward

THE COVE SCHOOL
Changing Lives. Building Futures.

350 Lee Road, Northbrook, Illinois 60062
Tel 847-582-2100 Fax 847-562-2112
www.coveschool.org

In 1947, little was known or understood about learning disabilities. Dr. Laura (Lehtinen) Rogan and Dr. Alfred A. Strauss emerged as pioneers in the field and began a movement that has influenced the field in profound ways. Their research led the way for others to better understand the unique population that challenged the ways educators thought and taught. Their studies proved that learning was possible for all, and their critical work gave students and families the hope they needed for a brighter future.

In 1947, with just a few children, a small rented space and a great determination to serve students who struggled to learn, the Cove School was born in Racine, Wisconsin.

The Cove School has moved several times since its inception. In 1950, Dr. Strauss maintained the residential site in Racine while Dr. Rogan opened the first Cove Day School in Evanston, IL. Both the residential and the day schools remained operational until the residential facility in Racine was closed permanently in 1968. Eventually, as enrollment grew, a high school program was added, and by the early 1980s, it became clear that more space was needed. Following several other moves to varying locations in northern Illinois, the Cove School moved to its current location at 350 Lee Road, Northbrook, IL.

Dr. Rogan was Clinical Director at Cove School until 1984. During that time, she conducted research, developed instructional materials, and educated professionals and parents. Her fundamental belief that you should never give up on a child led to this core philosophy that remains present at Cove today.

Cove currently serves approximately 170 students on its K-12 campus on Lee Road, and 24 students aged 18-22 at its Career Center in downtown Northbrook. Both sites provide students from diverse backgrounds with a highly individualized educational experience in a safe and respectful environment. Students come from all over the Chicagoland area to receive the specialized instruction that comes from our highly trained staff. Special education teachers and instructional assistants work closely with our clinical teams to provide an integrated approach to support the complex needs of our students. The clinical staff is extensive and includes speech and language pathologists, social workers, reading practitioners, occupational therapists, an art therapist, psychologist, and neuropsychologist. Class sizes are small which enables each student to receive individualized attention and customized instruction.

Through an integrated service delivery model, Cove is able to provide a holistic approach that embraces each student as a "whole child" while identifying the root cause for deficit remediation and the areas of strength for further development. Mental health support is embedded into the milieu and students are taught the strategies they need to build their social and emotional skills.

It is important at Cove that every student and family knows they belong. Community is valued and is an integral part of our shared success. The Cove Community is unique and continues to provide unwavering support and understanding for those who need us most.

Cove has transformed thousands of lives throughout the decades. We are forever grateful to our founder who set the vision, our families who believe in us, our incredible students who persevere and beat the odds, our dedicated staff who never give up, and our community who continuously support the work that we know must be done for those with disabilities.

I am deeply appreciative to all who have been part of our story. We've only just begun.

Sally L. Sover, Ed.D.
Executive Director

Preface:

The Cove Schools was the first of its kind in the nation—a school for those who (in 1947) were referred to as brain-injured children. My own difficulties are a pretty good cluster of the issues many Cove students were dealing with then: low IQ, poor coordination, medical conditions, hyperactivity, distractibility, behavioral issues, and learning disabilities. There were no programs, much less schools, for such students in Kentucky in the spring of 1962, though by the fall of 1962 a class for such children had been created in the Fayette County Public Schools system, Lexington, KY.

Consequently, it is important to point out that since this school was unique—the *only* school of its type in the United States—the school was performing a service by training both teachers how to teach and parents how to nurture their children. The Cove School is why I was able to write this book; to it, its faculty, staff, administrators, and students I give credit for all of my successes.

This memoir, "Yearnings," is written primarily in the form of a Japanese haibun—a form that utilizes a combination of prose and poetry. So clearly this is not an attempt at writing a traditional memoir. Neither is it a traditional haibun, particularly since it contains poems beyond just haiku, a burning haibun (after torrin a greathouse); even elephant jokes are included along with some family photographs. Yet I wrote this book largely in the haibun form because it is best able to help focus the story.

Please note that this memoir is built around many historical documents from the period 1948-

1966. These documents are letters written home, medical and educational records as well as family photographs. This is not a historical-based memoir with footnotes, properly sourced. Rather, it is a personal memoir written in prose and poetry and which often ignores the conventions of both.

However, for those uncomfortable with the lack of historical conventions, I expect that by the fall of 2025, all of the historical documents at the base of this book will be donated to the DeKoven Foundation in Racine, Wisconsin and at some point after their accessioning will be made available for use by scholars and historians.

Finally, readers are warned that there are 'errors' in this book due to the fact that some spelling conventions (class room, work books, etc.)

and grammar conventions have changed over time. In other instances, the spelling errors are due to the author's misspelling of words (Sonday instead of Sunday) in letters home (ages 7-11). In both instances corrections have not been made; there are neither in-text recognition of those errors nor footnotes. Please assume errors in this text exist for one of those reasons and that the author is the only person responsible for the inclusion of those errors in this work of creative nonfiction.

William H. McCann, Jr. MFA, MEd, MA
Winchester, KY 40391

Table of Contents

Introduction

Dr. Alfred A. Straus' Statement of Purpose for The
Cove Schools, 1948,
with Erasures: A Burning Haibun
(after torrin a greathouse)

The Cove Schools is a private residential school
(not for profit) for brain-injured children.
Specialized teaching methods are used, which have
been developed by the founders of the school in
order to meet the needs of these particular children.
Beyond the immediate goal of training the brain-
injured child by these special methods to assure his
more successful adjustment to his family, school
and community when he leaves The Cove Schools,
several other aims are served. The Cove Schools is
a training center for prospective teachers of brain-
injured children; it serves as a research unit for
enlarging our knowledge of these children; it seeks
to discover better methods in analyzing the
difficulties of the brain-injured child in the home,
school and the community. It wishes to stand as a
model for small boarding schools for this type of
child.

*

The staff of The Cove Schools considers the
enrollment of the child as a challenge for
developing him toward community adjustment. We,
therefore, maintain and strengthen the family ties.

Frequent visits by the parents are encouraged as soon as the child is adjusted in his new environment. Telephone calls between parents and child are recommended. Letters from parents and relatives and friends are a great help for the child's emotional growth. Restrictions are only imposed in the sending of packages. The full cooperation of the parents is necessary for our program and we, therefore, "enroll" parents for guidance and training into our school. The parents and the family must recognize and accept the challenge which a handicapped child imposes upon them during the stay of the child at the school and after his return to his home.

Alfred A. Strauss

*

The Cove Schools is a private residential school ▬▬▬▬▬▬ for brain-injured children. Specialized teaching methods are used ▬▬▬▬▬▬ ▬▬▬▬▬▬ in order to meet the needs of these particular children. ▬▬▬ the immediate goal of training the brain-injured child by these special methods ▬ assures his more successful adjustment to his family ▬▬▬ ▬▬▬▬ when he leaves The Cove Schools ▬▬▬▬▬▬ . The Cove Schools is a training center for ▬▬▬▬▬▬ brain-injured children; it serves as a research unit for enlarging our knowledge of these children ▬▬▬▬▬▬

and the community.

*

The staff of The Cove Schools considers the enrollment of the child as a challenge . We, therefore, maintain and strengthen the family ties. Frequent visits by the parents are encouraged . Telephone calls between parents and child are recommended. Letters from parents and relatives and friends are a great help for the child's emotional growth. The full cooperation of the parents is necessary for our program and we, therefore, "enroll" parents for guidance and training into our school. The parents accept the challenge which a handicapped child imposes upon them after his return to his home.

*

Cove Schools considers
        the child a challenge
Parents recognize a home.

The Cove Schools: My Life

The Gothic-styled school building on Lake
Michigan was near a beach, where fog and snow
        could wade ashore, and sometimes peer into
my room.

We were from east and west, north, and south:
        Sally's plastic horses roamed her dresser top
        Steve's mind roamed from weather to
stamps to chess…and more
        David's remote-controlled red sports car
with gull-wing doors was crashed and trashed
        One boy claimed to be The Lone Ranger's
nephew
        Dougie wore two hearing aids, turned up full
(and still couldn't hear)
        Joe's short-wave radio allowed us to listen
to *McHale's Navy* . . . once
        Susan liked the "Little Train Game"
        Steve, Joe, Tommy, David, and I were
roommates
        Another student bragged that his back yard
had a gold mine
        Tommy knew about hurricanes and told us
about living through some
        Steve knew about isobars and could explain
hurricanes
        Jaime, Seth, Steve, Tommy, and I were all in
the same Cub Scout den

On school days we watched *Bozo the Clown* at
noon, but once it wasn't funny:
        the president died that day in Dallas.

A few days later we watched the president's young
son salute his dad's casket as that son's sister
       walked sadly on . . . beside their mom.

For fun we rode sleds, had snowball fights, played
flashlight tag, and "50 All Scatter;"
       we flew kites, searched for sea glass, dug
holes, played basketball, and had fun.
       On TV were *Flipper*, *I Dream of Jeannie*,
Mr. Magoo, and *Walt Disney,* too.
       We screamed for the Beatles and our
favorite teams: Packers and Cubs
       We visited museums and zoos, and
Petrifying Springs, too.

But perhaps most of all, we students had each other:
       Steve, Joe, and I stayed up late to play
games or talk or sing, listen to the Cubs or Packers
games while others slept
       Early in the mornings we'd rise and talk and
dream…before we'd dine.
       We spoke of college and careers even as our
teachers and parents wondered if we were bright
enough to change a light bulb….
       College for us was a given.
       Though the adults we knew—unknown to
us—believed we'd be lucky to live in workshop
settings, certainly they did not believe we'd live on
our own.

I developed and lived up to my ABILITIES.
       I'd like to think my friends did, too.

Yearnings

Across the street from The Cove Schools was Lake Michigan. During the 1960s a sand beach was located where rocks and boulders, installed in 1978 to prevent erosion, now cover that beach. (Photo by the author, December 9, 2021)

1955: Mother's Day

[I was born May 8, 1955—Mother's Day—the oldest of what were to be six children of William H. McCann, Sr., a lawyer, and Betty Bruce Brown, a civic volunteer and housewife. My sister Laura was born in 1957. And until March 1959 things were 'good.' Laura and I were the first two. Those who followed were Sarah (1959), Bruce (1960), Susan (1962), and Elizabeth (1966).]

*

Just a perfect baby boy!
    Until . . . Nooo!
Why him? Why us? God?

*

1959: Falling Down

In March1959 when Bill Jr. fell I distinctly remember that it happened between the downstairs bathroom and our den and extra bedroom on St. Matilda Drive. And I think he was running, but maybe not. But I know I was standing in the dining room and witnessed what I at first thought was a fall. It was a seizure.

Perhaps a week later, I'm not certain, I remember Bill Jr. being in the hospital in Louisville and I spent the night with him and at that time—I believe it was nighttime. Bill was at home with Laura. And I remember that Dr. Roseman came in and told me the news about the type of seizures that Bill was experiencing. He was very abrupt and I was up practically the rest of the night crying, praying and just generally beside myself with fear, anxiety, and grief.

Bill had many grand mal seizures after the first one. I was with him daily—we didn't have extra help at the time—and he had combinations of all three seizures constantly. Even sitting right next to him, usually while he was on the floor since he couldn't walk with any ability to not fall—I still couldn't keep him from falling. And we, for some reason (maybe because it hadn't been suggested to us) did not put him in a football helmet till Oct. or Nov. 1959. The football helmet had a face guard.

*

Our son rose the sun
    Bright delight no more
Many problems ahead

*

[I didn't know it at the time but my sister, Sarah Inman McCann, was born December 12, 1959. She lived one hour.]

*

[Sarah was buried December 28, 1959. Two employees of Lexington Cemetery dug the grave, placed her small casket in the ground, and tamped the ground down. There was no ceremony. There would be no grave marker until Mother's Day, May 14, 2023.]

*

Sarah, would you . . . like us?
        Your five siblings.
We're not perfect.

*

1960: A Minister Ministers

January 6, 1960: Crestwood Christian Church, Lexington, Kentucky. Dear Bill and Boo Considering everything, maybe this isn't late, It is my desire to express my thanks for the gracious gift and to assure you that it is far above the demands of duty. Words do not come to say the deep and hidden feelings of our hearts when things go awry, We know what we wanted and are baffled when something else comes. It is an act of grace to be able to accept the unexpected, the undesired, and still be undefeated. I feel that both of you have achieved that level in your recent disappointment. My best to you for this year and that tomorrow. Sincerely, (signed) Jim (James A. Lollis, Minister)

*

[My brother Bruce was born in October 1960, at Central Baptist Hospital. He was five weeks premature, weighed 2 ½ pounds, and stayed in the pediatric ICU for two weeks before being allowed to go home. Eventually, he would be diagnosed with dyslexia, a learning disability.]

*

The wedding of my aunt and uncle—Eleanor Durall
and John Y. Brown, Jr. The author, ring
bearer, front and center, held in place by Uncle John.

1961: A Father Seeks Help

April 13, 1961: Dear Sir: My son William H. McCann, Jr. who will be six years of age on May 8, 1961, apparently has suffered brain damage as a result of Myoclonic Epilepsy[1] which began when he was about 3 years of age (March 2, 1958) and continued for about nine months. He is now attending Kindergarten and is also receiving tutoring one hour per week from Mr. Peggy Leiterman who has training and experience in the field of educating brain damaged children. Mrs. Leiterman is of the opinion that Bill has a perceptual deficit. She has suggested that we write you and request an evaluation of his condition and abilities. Bill was suffering almost constant Myoclonic seizures for about six months after his first attack. Prior to that time he was an exceptionally bright and alert child, Since that time he has been under medication and his improvement from the physical and emotional effects of this illness slow. We started him in nursery school in December 1959 and he continued there until June 1960. Since Sept. 1960 he has attended kindergarten. He is not functioning at kindergarten level, partially due, we feel, to the fact that his experience and learning were so limited during the period of his extreme illness and partially due to brain damage caused by the illness. He is cooperative, understands instructions, and has a reasonably good vocabulary, and now appears to be emotionally well adjusted. However, he shows lack of attention and a short attention span and other indications of brain damage. We understand it may

be possible to train parts of the brain to take over
the functions of the parts damaged and to greatly
improve his ability to learn by the use of proper
teaching methods. It is toward the end of obtaining
an evaluation of his ability and acquiring
information as to the best schools and teaching
methods for him that we are writing this letter. We
will appreciate what information you can furnish.
Sincerely [signed] William H. McCann

*

Knock, knock
        Who's there?
Banana who?

*

April 18, 1961: Dear Mr. McCann: Thank you for
your recent letter regarding an evaluation of your
son. I am very sorry to advise you that we do not do
any diagnostic or evaluative studies of children not
enrolled at the Cove Schools. Sincerely yours Laura
E. Lehtinen, Ph.D., Clinical Director

*

Hope lives in Racine
        In hearts conveyed in letters
Mercy: sought on 2-cent wings

*

The author, age six, May 1961, in the
backyard, Idle Hour Dr., Lexington, KY.
(Photographer unknown)

1962: Evidence of Change

January 11, 1962: Dear Mr. McCann: In response to
your recent inquiry, we are giving you the following
information. We accept in the day school brain-
injured children between the ages of six and twelve
years, but make exception if we feel the child may
make profit by our educational methods. The
children we accept may be educationally or
mentally retarded.[2] The important factor for the
decision to as to enrollment is whether the child will
so profit within a reasonable time of a few years
that he may attend a public school. Furthermore
from the behavior standpoint, the child should be
able to attend a day school and it should be to his
advantage to live at his own home, We do not
accept children who will need custodial care now or
later in life, nor do we enroll children with seizures.
For the decision of enrollment it is necessary to

have a medical report diagnosing the brain injury, a
psychologist's report, and school reports if the latter
are available.

THE COVE SCHOOLS

*

Cove messages request
    No custodians need apply
Must give evidence of change

*

Knock, knock
Who's there?
Banana

Knock, knock
Who's there
Banana
Banana who?

*

MEDICAL EVALUATION AND
RECOMMENDATION: William McCann

January 16, 1962: Ephraim Roseman, M.D.
Louisville, KY Dear Dr. Strauss: I understand that
you are contemplating the enrollment of William
McCann of Lexington, Ky. in your residential;
school. I am very grateful to you for doing this,
since I certainly feel that William McCann offers a
good possibility from the standpoint of being
helped. I have known him since April 1, 1958, and
saw him because of the fact that he was having
myoclonic seizures. As you know, these are usually
very difficult seizures to get under control and
frequently cause brain damage, However,
fortunately, his seizures have been well controlled
and he has had none since Jan. 1959. He has, of
course, had some brain damage but I am impressed
by the fact that this has been comparatively small. I
should like to emphasize that he has had no seizures
since and that his general health has been excellent.
The only medication he has required is that of
Mysoline and phenobarbital. Furthermore, presently
we are in the process of reducing his medication so
that we expect to have him off of all forms within 1
$^{1/2}$-2 years. If I can be of any further help at any
time, I shall consider it a pleasure if you would let
me know. With best wishes and great hopes that
you will accept him in your school, I am, Sincerely,
[signed] E. Roseman, M.D.

*

Doctors worked overtime
        Even minds can be wasted, or not
Mine was saved, restored

*

WILLIAM H. MCCANN, JR: EVALUATION OF EDUCABLE STATUS

February 14, 1962: University of Kentucky Medical
Center, Confidential Medical Information
Gentlemen: I am writing you at the request of Mr.
William H. McCann of Lexington, Kentucky, in
regard of his son, William H. McCann, Jr. We saw
William H. McCann, Jr. in the early summer of
1961 at the request of his father for an evaluation of
his educable status. The parents expressed concern
over planning for his future. The mother indicated
considerable tension and even some exasperation
over what she viewed "Bill's demands" upon
certain repetitive problems. These seem to fall into
two main complaints; one, that he needed to be in
frequent contact with her physically as well as in
sight if she were at home; and two, that he was quite
insistent that every object be in its place, If things
were left out he would immediately return it to the
place that it ordinarily was kept, and that unless the
object was in immediate use, he was quite persistent
until things were in order. Our over-all impression
was that the father was more reconciled and
accepting of the result of the illness of the child than
was the mother at this time. Our impression was
that this child, of course, does have brain damage

from his past history of myoclonic epilepsy which has miraculously become well controlled. He was eager to learn and to attempt to excel and acutely sensitive to failures. He is quite cooperative during examinations, but did exhibit the tendency of many organic children for some physical contact and an obsessive-like need to have everything in its place, There was no evidence of autistic behavior[3] or thought processes, Interview with the parents indicate that there is some discrepancy between the mother and the father's acceptance of the child's limitations that his illness has created for him. This was exemplified by the mother's placing the child in a nursery school the previous year with a reputation for taking "very quick and bright children." It was our impression that Bill is certainly trainable and educable within reasonable limits. I hope that Bill can have the special training that he needs. Yours sincerely, [signed] Joseph B. Parker, Jr. M.D., Professor and Chairman

*

Knock, knock
Who's there
Banana
Banana who

Knock, knock
Who's there?
Orange
Orange who?
Orange you glad I didn't say banana?

*

REPORT OF THE EVALUATION COMMITTEE,
UNITED CEREBRAL PALSY OF THE
BLUEGRASS, RE: WILLIAM H. MCCANN, JR.

February 14, 1962: United Cerebral Palsy of the
Bluegrass, Executive Office, Mrs. Rhea A. Taylor,
Director Dear Mrs. Strauss: Mr. & Mrs. William
McCann requested us to submit copies of reports
from our Evaluation Committee but each
professional member wished to send a report
directly to you. Mr. & Mrs. McCann are highly
intelligent cultured people of the upper socio-
economic group in our community. They have three
children of whom William, Jr. born May 8, 1955 is
the oldest. Bill has shown so much and response in
the 2-2 $^{1/2}$ hour daily program we provide that we
believe he will rapidly progress in a 24 hour daily
structured experience. In his home environment
there cannot be complete consistency and there are
many frustrations. The parents are eager and willing
to do what is best for Bill, but we all know that
there are many home situations that cannot be
changed by a mere wish. Mrs. McCann has
faithfully attended a Mother's discussion group and
Mr. McCann has started with a recently organized
Father's discussion group. Their participation
reveals a great interest, a little insight, and much
eagerness to learn more in order to be helpful to
their children. These sessions are being conducted
in accordance with the Child Study Association of
America plan. Mr. and Mrs. McCann, I feel sure, if
you encourage them that during Bill's absence they
may be able to develop some changes

(unconsciously) perhaps, and, therefore, understand him better. We do hope you can accept him in your program. Sincerely, [signed] Mrs. Rhea A. Taylor, Director, UCPB

*

EDUCABILITY EVALUATION, CHILD GUIDANCE SERVICES, LEXINGTON, KY, RE: WILLIAM H. MCCANN, JR.

February 23, 1962: Child Guidance Service, Lexington, KY Gentlemen: We have been advised that Bill McCann is being considered for admission to your school and at the request of his parents we are placing at your disposal all of the information that we have obtained through our contacts with the child. We first saw Bill McCann on July 23, 1959. He was referred to us on July 13, 1959 with request for an evaluation of the levels of his intellectual and emotional maturity. It was thought at that time that such information might contribute toward making educational plans for him. It was at that time that we learned that Bill suffered seizures and had been placed on anti-convulsive medication by Dr. Ephraim Roseman, General Hospital, Louisville, Kentucky. Bill, accompanied by his mother was seen on July 23, 1959, at which time an effort was made to administer the Revised Stanford-Binet Scale, Form L. Although at the time four years and two months of age, appeared sturdy in respect to his over-all physical status, he nevertheless evinced extreme awkwardness, clumsiness, and poor coordination of bodily movements. His speech was slurred, fluctuated in volume and, at times, Bill seemed impaired in his articulation by accumulations of saliva in his mouth; there was considerable drooling. We found it difficult to elicit this child's attention and keep him focused on the tasks, We noted that he frequently perseverated and was unable to break a previous set in order to meet the demands of a new task. Our last contact with Bill McCann was on August 18, 1961, at which time the Revised Stanford-Binet Scale, Form L was re-administered. Bill's effort and attention were much better focused and sustained than previously. He was cooperative and quite willing to participate in "playing the games." He was apprehensive of failure, reluctant to venture, and disposed to distrust himself when confronted with tasks that were relatively difficult for him. In contrast with this, his social confidence seemed normal for his age and he had no difficulty interacting with either children or adults. He was vulnerable to distracting influences, particularly those in his immediate physical and social environment.

*

Merciful teachers
        Seeking help for one
May find hope for many

*

[March 9, 1962: Early morning. *Daddy, where are we? Where are we going, Daddy?* We're in Indianapolis. We'll get there soon. It's pretty when the sun comes up. *It is. Mommy's asleep?* Yes. Aren't you tired, Bill? *A little bit. Not much. I'm a big boy now.* True. But your mommy's asleep. It's okay for big boys to sleep when Mommy's sleeping. *Oh. Ok. I think I'll go back to sleep then.* Good night, big boy. *'Night, Daddy.*]

*

I watched with envy
 •   Others throw snowballs with glee
Sick, I watched in misery

*

March 15, 1962: We were four small boys sharing a room far from familiar homes, far from protective parents. I raised the shade. There was no sun to enter our room with inviting warmth. Instead, from off the Lake came a dense fog, on "little cat feet" sneaking up on us—rolling relentlessly closer and closer until—it didn't. The fog stopped just out of reach, if the window was open. We are safe—any tentacles hidden in the fog stay right there—right where they can't reach us. "Breakfast, boys!" We hurried out, scurried to the siren call of a breakfast of hot cereal, buttered toast, and milk. So we ignored any danger from a fog no longer beckoning us to stray outside where the fog might have hidden us from the safety of teachers and friends new and old.

Cove Schools building. Now DeKoven Foundation
Racine, Wisconsin
(photo taken by author 2023)

Racine, WI Zoo, circa 1962, Dad and me
(Mom's the photographer)

*

Hello, I'm Joe
       Will you be my pal
Always, and for life

*

[Initially, there was one thing strange about meals at
Cove Schools: pushers. Not drug pushers. Not
bullies pushing me around. But an extra utensil at
each place setting. Besides knives and forks and
spoons, each place setting had a 'pusher'—an
aluminum instrument a few inches long and a
couple of inches high at one end that looked, more
or less, like a rake without tines. It was solid on that
end and could be used to push things like peas, or
rice, or corn, or whatever else onto a fork or spoon.
And for someone like me who had trouble with
balance and perceptual problems, the pusher was a
real help.]

*

New and far away? Scary.
       New friends can be nice, fun even.
But home would be better

*

March 20, 1962: Dear Mommie and Daddy. Susan and I are playing the *Little Train Game.* Maybe I'll win this time. Holly is being noisy. She is making a lot of noise. Saturday and Sunday we had fun playing. I played outdoors today, My cold is all gone. I took a nap at rest time. Sally has a new toy watch. I'm ahead in my game with Susan. Billy J. has a model ship that he made. Love and kisses. Billy

*

March 27, 1962: Susan and I are playing a game called *Pollyanna.* Memom sent me a letter. I like school fine. We had movies Sunday. Mr. Olson ran the movie projector. We saw movies of birds, and animals, and fish. Saturday we had candy for a treat and Sunday we had cookies. Dougie got a red flying parachute in the mail from his mommie. Today we flew flying saucers, mine went high up and very far. Love and kisses Bill.

*

Delicate white bells
     Atop tender green shoots
Silently ring in spring

*

April 11, 1962: Dear Mommie and Daddy. We got up early yesterday morning. We boarded a big orange school bus and went to Chicago. We saw ducks, pigs and a farm. I saw how baby chicks come out of eggs. We saw a lake, a dam, and rain. When it thundered and lightninged, it was really loud; I got scared. I saw a lot of strange machines, even a submarine! We went in a coal mine to see how they get coal. Then we saw coal burn. It burns bright and hot, just like wood. At lunch we all ate in the cafeteria. Mr. Bartlett needed my help I got napkins for the other children, just like a big boy. I had a good time in Chicago. Going back to school—past fields and homes, just like we have in Lexington—I fell asleep. Love and kisses Bill

*

Chicago is huge!
      Big, cold, scary, and so much fun
Is life that way, too?

*

April 28, 1962: Ephraim Roseman, MD., Louisville KY. Re: Wm. McCann, Lexington, KY. Dear Sir: At the suggestion of Mrs. McCann I am sending you copies of prescriptions for her son, William. He is taking 1 ½ tablet of Mysoline each day. Each tablet contains 250 mgm. He also takes 3 tablets of phenobarbital one day and 4 the next day alternately. Each tablet contains ½ grain. If I can furnish any further information, please let me know. Sincerely, (signed)   E. Roseman, M.D.

*

May 8, 1962: I'm seven! I'm a big boy now.

*

Why did the elephant paint its toenails red?
        So it could hide in a cherry tree.

*

May 14, 1962: From my window I can see a large
tree across the driveway that has a hollow place in
it. Shaped like a witches' hat, the space inside it
looks like it might be a home for elves. Maybe Joe
or Steve know if the Cove has elves.

*

Do elves live in trees?
        Do elves go to school like me?
I have much to learn.

*

Bill McCann. Spring 1962.

Bill has been in the classroom now for a little over a month. He came only for the morning program for the first two weeks taking a nap in the afternoon, More recently he has attended class both morning and afternoons. Bill is being taught some of the group activities that the children participate in such as working with blocks, telling the day of the week, giving the date, observing the weather, etc. He is open to these activities but needs to learn such things as waiting his turn, raising his hand and staying in his seat. He is settling down but at times is quite obstinate in resisting directions. "I am not going to do what you say." Or "I don't have to if I don't want to." He can generally be talked around. At his desk he does puzzles of ten to fifteen pieces occasionally asking for help. He has done peg designs thru holes in tagboard and designs reduced in size by tagboard masks. In the past two weeks he has begun to do simple peg designs from a design on another board or on paper. These designs are around the edges of the board. He has great difficulty in drawing the figures that he has made but has been successful with straight lines and squares. He does not care for free drawing and to date has only made an airplane.

Charles H. Bartlett

*

[Mr. Bartlett was tall and friendly, not tall and intimidating (like my dad could be). He was principal of the Cove Schools in Racine, though I didn't find that out until 2021, when I read materials supplied to me by librarians at the Racine Public Library. If anything, at the time, I think I thought that Mr. Olson was in charge, because he was there every Sunday afternoon to show movies in his classroom, which was the largest of the four.

[Instead, I found out that Mr. Bartlett was the principal. And from the local city directories I also found out that he had lived in the Gatehouse each of the four years I attended school there.

[After the school closed in June 1968, he visited my family and me for dinner. I remember sitting next to him at the dinner table, very proud that he would visit us in Lexington. Turned out he was headed to Knoxville, TN to interview to enter a doctoral program in Education.

[He either didn't like the program or wasn't accepted because he didn't go to school there. Instead, he got his degree from Northwestern. Eventually, he retired from the University of Cincinnati as full Professor and a former director of the Children's Center for Developmental Disorders.]

*

Bill McCann. June 1962.

Since Easter Bill has gained in his ability to handle visual-perceptual materials. He is now able to do simple peg designs that are around the outer edge of the board as well as diagonal lines, He can do vertical block designs of several pieces and places parquetry blocks directly on top of the designs. All that bill writes is his name in capital letters and the numbers 1, 4, 6, 7, and 9. He often writes his name backwards as well as reversing the numbers that he writes. Since putting his name up on the wall before his desk he does a little better. He uses his right hand for tracing and such writing as he does. Exercises and other classroom activities must be demonstrated for him. Verbal explanations that accompany such demonstrations mean little to him. He often looks puzzled and will say, "I don't know what you mean." Or he will go ahead and make a mistake and then say, "I didn't know what to do." He doesn't want to make mistakes and feels bad about it when he does, Although there are reports of his hitting other children he gets along all right when occupied with materials in the classroom and there is no adverse interaction with the children.

Charles H. Bartlett

*

[Games were always fun, something I looked forward to, enjoyed all four years in Racine. In the first two letters home I mentioned games, "The Little Train Game" and "Pollyanna." But other games were mentioned in later letters—chess, "Monopoly"—in reports written about me—'Bill likes "Civil War" and chess'—and in memories, of playing cribbage almost every morning with Joe or Steve, and of playing "Parcheesi" on the (netless) tennis court.]

*

Rock, paper, scissors
     Does God play children's games?
Do adults play God's games?

*

June 15, 1962: Mr. Olson took me to O'Hare Airport to fly home. That's in Chicago. I remember how he was so tall and walked so fast—or so it felt to me—through the airport. When we got to my gate—he took me on the plane and introduced me to the stewardess and the captain. They showed me around the cockpit—"where I fly the plane," the captain explained. Later, after lifting me onto a seat, Mr. Olson left after saying, "You're in good hands, Bill. Have a good trip" The plane was a DC-3. A small plane by modern standards, to me it seemed huge: my short legs stuck straight out; I couldn't bend them, much less feel the floor. Time flew by. The engine roared. The plane took off. I saw clouds outside the window. Soon the captain said we would be landing. Gently, like a hen settling on a nest, the plane landed at Bowman Field in Louisville and I would soon be home. Boy, was it great to see Mom and Dad again, sister Laura and brother Bruce, too.

*

June 16, 1962: So good to be home. Mom had a party for me, a 'Welcome Home, Bill' party. The hats and cake and kids were over—and they were great. We had a good party. But soon after it was over some of the neighbors started teasing me, chasing after me with a stick that they had put catsup on—they called it mean blood—and shouting, "Mean blood! Mean blood is gonna get you, Billy boy!" The summer would be long.

*

DC-3s are huge
          when one is only four-feet tall
small: when a wide adult

*

September 7, 1962: Good to see my friends again. But I'll miss the elves. The door to their home is filled with concrete. I hope they're safe.

*

September 8, 1962, Dad gave me his rank bars and other things he had from the Army. I put them inside my pillowcase last night just before I went to sleep. When I woke up, they were still there. It was like Dad was there to comfort me.

*

[The Cove only used part of the building it was
housed in. The rest of the building was a convent. I
don't recall seeing a single nun while living there.
Indeed, the whole building was three blocks long,
I'm guessing, and only about a third of the building
was occupied by the school. Whether or not anyone
actually lived or worked in the rest of building was
anyone's guess. However, there was a basement.
And in one of the bedrooms on the boys' side of the
building was a dumbwaiter which we could access
from that room. We could open the door to access
the dumbwaiter. But no one ever had the courage to
get in it and go down because we couldn't be
certain of what lay beneath us, or if we'd ever be
able to get out/up.]

*

September 15, 1962: When I went to bed Dad's
stuff was missing from my pillow case. I don't
know what happened to it. But I had a hard time
falling asleep.

*

[Besides the main building, there were other features and buildings on the grounds. Most noticeable was the black six-foot chain link fence that encircled the entire grounds. Though there are more entries now, when I lived at the Cove there was only a single gate, located, naturally enough, at the Gate House. Besides that, there were a couple of other buildings on the grounds that I had not been in until December 2021, when current DeKoven Foundation executive director Lynn Biess-Carol gave my wife and me a tour of the buildings on the grounds, other than the one I lived in as a child when it was the Cove Schools, Racine.

[Additionally, there was a tennis court on the grounds and an outdoor brick grill with a semi-circular brick bench. The tennis court did not have a net (and we were too uncoordinated to play tennis anyway) but I do remember at least one instance of playing "Parcheesi" on a warm late-spring day there with a few other students, and probably an adult. And of the outdoor grill, the letters home document an outdoor picnic. But the main features of the grounds were the main building, which I always described as being very similar to Madeline's home in Paris—where 12 little girls went everywhere in two straight lines, the youngest of whom was Madeline—and the spacious grounds that surrounded it all.

[That first fall in Racine, Halloween was celebrated by going door to door in the neighborhood surrounding the school. My friends and I were

dressed in costumes, properly equipped with paper
bags or plastic buckets and supervised, and all of us,
princesses or spacemen, cowboys and many others
no doubt went around yelling, "Trick or Treat" and
coming away with lots of candy. That first
Halloween was lots of fun!]

*

Christmas is joy.
		Halloween is costumed fun
Trick or Treat dentist's delight

*

December 8, 1962: Bill McCann is enjoying the work in the pre-primers. We have just finished *We Look and See* and *We Work and Play* and his attitude toward reading is good. He frames words easily and reads to find answers to questions I ask. We usually take just one page a day but every once in a while, Bill will ask if we can't do the next page, too, and so, every so often, we do another page. A number of times he has asked to take the book to his desk, then he has studied a page and read it to me (with help) He is interested in library books and has read pages in *Ned and Nancy* (with help). He is building a sight vocabulary which includes the colors, names of numbers, days of the week, everyday words used in teacher made stories and seat work and words found in the work books he uses. Bill has to be helped quite a bit with his number work because he isn't too interested in concentrating on numbers. He adds up to the sum of six and subtracts from six. He writes the numbers to ten and I usually dot the five and eight, but some time ago he called out, "I can make the 5 and I can make the 8." He was doing well with no copy at all, However the next day he had to have it dotted again. Now he is making the 5 with no help, for his problems often add up to five, but he says, "I make it too big." He fills blanks before and after number, but I put the numbers 1 to 10 across the top of the page so he can refer to them. He likes to use the print set for this type of exercise. He arranges numbers easily to 30. He is very good on the magnetic board work, We work with the numbers, names of numbers, and dot configurations to 10.

Bill's attitude toward his school work is very good.
There are times he acts a little immature—slouches
on his chair, tries to bother Billy, wants to see what
others are doing, talks out loud—but generally he is
there to work and does work to the best of his
ability. He fairly radiates pride as he carefully adds
another piece of completed work to little "pile for
the day—and how pleased he is when he selects
some of it to take in and show Mrs. Strauss.

Edith De Moulpied

*

[Mrs. De Moulpied was 50 years old when I started at the Cove Schools, and so very kind. She was interested in her students and sought to encourage us. She also had an interest in gardening that came across through her showing us how to grow sweet potatoes hydroponically. And then on another occasion she showed us how to plant wheat. But what I remember best was the day when both Mrs. Schwager and Mr. Olson were both absent.

[Mrs. De Moulpied looked out the window and noticed, I kid you not, an Indy 500 race car parked across the street from the school. Well, of course, everyone wanted to see the car. So with her in the lead, we walked out the Gatehouse Gate, turned left and walked up toward the car. She made us stop at the corner—across from the car—then when she said it was safe we ran pell-mell toward the car. She wouldn't let us get in the car or do any more than look, but I haven't been as close to an Indy car as I was that day.]

*

Christmas oh Christmas
      Angels We Have Heard on High
Do they sing on key?

*

1963: Standing Up

January 14, 1963: Ephraim Roseman, M.D.
Louisville, KY Re: William McCann
Dear Mrs. Strauss: I have been asked by the father o
William McCann to write you about Bill's
medication. We are, of course, gradually taking him
off all medication. For the present he has
discontinued the Mysoline and he is to continue to
take three tablets of phenobarbital one day and the
next day alternately. Each tablet contains one-half
grain. At the end of each three months the
medication will be reduced by one-half pill. If I can
furnish additional information please let me know.
                    Sincerely, E. Roseman, M.D.

*

January 20, 1963: It's cold. Just 18°. The wind and
snow are blowing hard, so we stayed inside. We had
recess in the gym on the third floor. I hope that the
whole winter won't be like this. I don't like the
cold. But I like to play in the snow. Tommy likes
cold even less, he's from Charleston, a town on a
sea, where he said, "it's never this cold." But he
likes playing in the snow, too.

*

[I don't know why but Steve and Joe and I had late bedtimes. We got to stay up an hour longer than anyone else. We'd roam the second floor offices and rooms. We'd play "Monopoly" or "Parcheesi" or read. Sometimes we'd do things together. But just as often we'd go our separate ways. When I went off, I liked to read. Sometimes I'd play music. But my favorite thing was to read a story in a *Childcraft* book in Mr. Olson's room or search out a *Hardy Boys* mystery, or maybe a *Tom Swift* adventure. These were my first feelings of independence and I loved it!]

*

February 13, 1963: One thing I really enjoy is reading. Books in Mr. Olson's room include *Childcraft* books, *The Hardy Boys, Best in Children's Books,* and *Tom Swift*. I don't always understand what I read. When that happens I ask questions of my friends or teachers or other adults. The world is so big, so interesting and I want to learn everything I can about everything I can.

*

Hardy Boys find trouble
    Solving mysteries together
Can I do that, too?

*

March 11, 1963: Dear Mom and Dad, I am sending you some of my good work. Saturday was "A Day in Town Day" we had money and we could buy things. I bought a telephone and some candy. Sunday we had movies. One was about butterflies, another was about wildlife. It was snowing very hard outdoors. We went out to play in it for awhile. Mike went out with his parents this weekend. How is our baby Susan? Does she have any teeth yet? Did you send me my Silly Putty and scotch tape yet? Maybe its on its way. Love and kisses Bill

*

Lake winds blew cold snow
    It piled in around us deep
Perfect for snowball games

*

March 11, 1963: Law Offices of Brown, Sledd & McCann Dear Mrs. Strauss: Mrs. McCann and I are planning to attend the Fund for Perceptually Handicapped conference at the LaSalle Hotel on April 6. We would then like to visit with Bill on Sunday and Monday and possibly Tuesday morning. I trust that it will not interfere too greatly to take him out school part of the time, We would of course visit on the weekend, but feel it is important to attend the conference, and, accordingly, plan to change our plans to include one day at Chicago. Please advise immediately if these arrangements are not satisfactory Bill's birthday is May 8. Rather than mail a gift to him we will probably bring them up there on this occasion and let you hold them for his birthday. If you have suggestions for an appropriate gift, we would appreciate receipt of that in the near future in order that we can purchase something for him that you feel would be appropriate and beneficial for him. Enclosed is a check for $500 for the payment[4] due March 15. With kindest regards I am, Very truly yours

(signed) WILLIAM H. McCANN

*

[What a cold winter that was. At the same time, I remember what a good time we had playing in the snow. One game we played was to make a large spoked wheel, a group of us tromping out the design. It was—I'm guessing now—that the path was maybe three feet wide, all around the wheel and in the inner spokes as well. So maybe the wheel's circumference was 20 feet or more across. Then we played "tag"—but those who were "it" and those trying to get away had to stay on the paths that had been trampled into the snow.]

*

Brisk snow, crisply thrown
        snowballs hit trees missing me
When I am lucky

*

April 1, 1963: Dear Mom & Dad, Sunday we flew kites. Peter has a kite that looks like a long balloon. It looks almost like a rocket ship. It can't go around the earth. But we had a lot of fun flying it. We saw movies yesterday. My favorite one showed men making steel. They would pour it as a liquid. And magically it would become a solid that you could hit with a hammer. It was cool. Sunday we had chocolate milk and animal crackers for our treat. There is a fog outdoors that feels bad and it has been raining. I'm going to art now, and I am going to make a bank. We could not go out for recess because it was raining and really foggy this morning. I couldn't see the lake. Love and kisses Bill

*

[I've always been an early riser. Steve and Joe and I—and after Joe left, Tommy—woke up early every morning. Sometimes a game of cribbage might break out. But always we would talk about what we were going to do when we left the Cove, where we'd go to college, what we'd major in, the jobs we wanted to have, our career paths forward. Steve's dad was a doctor in Hartford, CT; he wanted to follow in his dad's footsteps. My dad was a lawyer. I really didn't want to do that, but I knew I'd succeed. If you come from a family of successful people, isn't success a given? We all thought so. We also planned to be successful. That helped, too.]

*

April 6, 1963: Often in our phonics works we write the beginning letter under the picture and recently Bill will say, "I wrote the "l" or the "r", I didn't print it. And sure enough, he had made some very good ones. It was quite the day when he wrote his name. He takes great pride in the fact that he is writing and just beginning to put a few letters together as "it", and "me" Bill enjoys phonics work and is very good at picking out beginning sounds. He is getting the idea of th ending sounds and has done a little rhyming. We have used several Science books—Look and Learn, and All Around US" and I have found Bill is quite observing, giving normal responses you would expect from a child his age. He enjoys the calendar work, the put-together surprise picture on Friday—never a piece upside down now, and very neatly pasted together, With help, he assembles the sentence story of three or four words under the picture and pastes it on. Bill is alert and eager to do his assignments. His attitude is good and he is proud when he does a good piece of work.

Edith De Moulpied

*

My kite out of sight
    Snapped string suddenly
Falls sadly to the ground

*

June 5, 1963: Academic Report Bill McCann
<u>Arithmetic</u> Bill counts and writes the numbers by ones from 1-30. He has some difficulty putting in missing numbers especially of it is the number before. Bill has the dot configurations from 1-6 well established in his mind. Beyond the 6 pattern, I'm not sure how well he knows them. Visualizing the dot patterns on his desk is very difficult for him. The combinations made from these patterns are not firmly established. <u>Writing</u> He is doing very well in writing. The x and z are the only lower case letters he is unsure of. As yet, he has learned no capitals, Connecting an o to another letter gives him some trouble. He writes from a copy. Bill is a good worker. He stays at his work until it is finished, even though he may have some trouble, he never gets discouraged. Sometimes he copies the actions or repeats things he sees or hears but he generally can be quieted in a short time. Otherwise Bill is relatively quiet in the classroom.

Mrs. Schwager

*

[The same day Mrs. Schwager and Mr. Olson were absent, Mrs. De Moulpied took us to the beach across the street from the school to see the Indy racing car before she introduced us to sea glass. Worn smooth by waves and water, sand and friction, sea glass is glass made beautiful—smooth and beautiful—by the effects of time and Lake Michigan's waves and tides. Once Mrs. De Moulpied introduced sea glass to us—and we were able to find some for ourselves—I for one wanted to find more of it. When they came for a visit once, I got Mom and Dad to explore the beach with me, looking for sea glass.]

*

June 22, 1963: Laura swims like a fish. Two years younger and she can swim back and forth across the swimming pool. She can even swim in the deep end. I swim like a rock.

*

July 4, 1963: We went to the beach. Aunt Jane and Uncle Mac and their kids upstairs, Dad and Mom, Laura, Bruce, Susan, and me downstairs. Today Laura and I made a huge sandcastle. Later, Bruce kicked it and messed it up. I didn't like that. Once it got dark we lit sparklers and ran around on the beach like little suns or something.

*

July 5, 1963: Dad taught Laura to body surf. But I can't swim. So I could only stand on the beach and watch. What a lonely feeling.

*

Swimming must be fun
          I know I don't like just watching
I want in the game

*

July 25, 1963: Mom is teaching me to swim. That's what she calls it. But mostly I make splashes when my arms smack the water.

*

September 15, 1963: (handwritten and unsigned)
Bill McCann Very good summer, no organized
program. Now good friends with his sister. Asks
many questions sometimes because he's confused,
sometimes because he wants attention. Occasionally
Bill gets stubborn. Even less often he'll throw a
tantrum. Parents seems to be handling him generally
very well.

*

September 25, 1963: Dear Mom and Dad Today we
played a game called "Jump the Candle Stick" it
was fun to play. We had music today. We marched,
galloped, played "Ten Little Indians" and sang
songs. The music teacher had a monkey puppet. The
monkey was frightened and hid his face on the
teacher's shoulder. He was frightened because we
were noisy. He washed his face and hands. He had
something in a bag. Guess what it was, it was a
giant toothbrush. He was fun to watch. Last night
we played games, "50 All Scatter" and "Spud." It's
time to go back to school and work hard. Love and
kisses Bill

*

High in leafless tree
        sat a sea bird hidden
From my camera's eye

*

November 22, 1963: I didn't understand why CBS News interrupted *Bozo the Clown* to talk about the president, who was in Dallas. "We interrupt this program to announce that President Kennedy has been shot...." I didn't know what a president was. But no one turned off the television. No one changed the channel. I don't remember anyone saying anything, doing anything. Though moments before we had been laughing at Bozo's antics, now we were somber, and none of us more than 10. We watched the announcement of the president's death. We watched as the new president took the oath of office standing next to the blood-wearing widow. None of us cried. But we all understood that someone had died and that adults around us were shocked. No doubt, some of them cried.

*

November 23, 1963: I read a story in *Childcraft* about John Wilkes Booth, the assassin of Abraham Lincoln, tonight. In the story Booth was burned alive in a Virginia barn while Union soldiers tried to get him to come out of the barn. Later, I went to bed and though I tossed and turned a bit, I fell asleep. But it was a restless sleep and I had a dream where I saw Booth burned alive in that barn. And I heard his screams. It was so vivid. It was like I was there watching the Union troops setting fire to the barn, and of the sounds of the assassin trying to escape. I don't remember dreams. This may well be the only dream I ever remember. I woke up sweaty and scared. So I got up out of bed. After going to the bathroom, I stopped at the desk of the night watchwoman. She is there to keep us safe every night. And the *Chicago Tribune* with pictures and articles about the death of the president was folded beside her. But she was playing a card game. So I sat down by her desk and told her about my dream. I told her that the dream scared me. We sat there a few minutes and talked about the story, about President Kennedy. Then I asked her what she was doing. "I'm playing solitaire. Would you like to learn how to play, too?" "Sure." So she showed me how to play solitaire and a little later I went back to bed and soon fell asleep.

*

November 25, 1963: They buried the president
today and all of us watched the ceremony on
television. All of it. We saw the president's young
son—who was younger than any of us—salute the
president's flag-draped casket as it rolled by on a
horse-drawn wagon. We watched the riderless horse
with boots turned backwards lead the procession,
the widow with a black veil covering her face, her
children, her brothers-in-law and others; they all
walked solemnly behind the caisson. Narrating and
explaining it all was news anchor Walter Cronkite
who explained it well enough that I understood it
all.

*

Walter Cronkite talks
    Bozo the Clown's joy no more
President dead in Dallas

*

December 9, 1963:   Bill McCann asked me if he couldn't have "I Work by Myself." "Didn't you do that last year?, I asked him. "Yes," he said. "You had to explain things to me. Now I know that I can do it all by myself. So he got the book and is thoroughly enjoying it. It's a pleasure to watch him work in it. Bill is a pleasure to work with. He has a strong desire to learn and works to the best of his ability. He is very cooperative and been a wonderful help to me in helping get Mike adjusted to our situation. It is wonderful to see how Bill has matured.

Edith De Moulpied

*

December 10, 1963: <u>Arithmetic</u> Bill counts and writes by ones, the numbers from 1-100. He knows the dot configurations from 1-10 and knows some of the addition and subtraction combinations made from those patterns. Bill has a set of cards with the 7, 8, 9, 10 pattern on them which he uses when he does his arithmetic seat work. Some days he gets along fine while other times he has great difficulty and needs help. Bill performs much better in a group than he does independently. Writing Bill can write in cursive hand all the lower and many of the upper case letters. His writing is done skillfully but laboriously. Being able at last to copy his letter to his parents from a pattern is a big achievement for him. It is truly a pleasure to have Bill in my classroom. He works slowly but steadily until his work is completed, Some Days, Bill forgets completely how to do things that have been mechanical to him other days. He gets quite upset on those days. He works puzzles if he has any spare time.

Mrs. Schwager

*

[Mrs. Schwager was older than I guess everyone at the Cove School, except Mrs. Strauss. In 1962 she was 55 years old and until 2021 I did not know her first name: Laurel. Of course, I and the other students called all of the adults by the title of Mr., Mrs., or Miss—but we did know their first names. So far as I know, though, none of us kids knew Mrs. Schwager's first name. But that didn't matter then or now because she was a wonderfully kind person and a good teacher. She is also the person who wrote those first letters home for me. I wonder if she ever considered it an imposition to take dictation from a six-year-old?]

*

Weekly letters home
    Told of days at Cove
Mom's memory markers

*

December 10, 1963: MOTOR PROGRAM I feel our students are receiving benefits from our motor program. They are all showing better coordination and rhythm—moving just a bit easier; a little bit more sure of themselves as they balance on the plank and balancing board. Douggie and Rick seem to just "bound ahead" taking things right in stride and coming up with new ideas which they enjoy trying. Bill McCann shows dogged persistence as he works at the step-up board. It was very distressing for him at first but he is mastering it and his movement is becoming easier. I'm wondering about something, There are days that Bill reads much smoother and writes easier. Is that also one of his good motor program days. Mike shows the most improvement of all. He had to start at the bottom, so to speak, couldn't skip, couldn't even remember how to gallop, timid on the 2x4, afraid of the "flying bag" but he is now coming right along and showing "bits" of improvement. Thinking of Mike, here's a thought—pretty "far-fetched." His work in the classroom shows improvement—is this a carryover from the motor program? Time will tell if this program will help our pupils become more adequate and able to adjust to their environment. I think it will.

Edith De Moulpied

*

Home for holidays
     Christmas cheer, fun, & presents!
Missing "Happy New Year" cheers

*

What time is it when an elephant sits on a fence?
     Time to fix the fence.

*

1964: My Life in Letters

January 12, 1964: Steve collects stamps and he's
got me interested in stamp collecting, too. And on
Christmas I got a stamp album from my parents that
has been a lot of fun. Steve and I often work on our
albums together. We trade stamps. We talk about
the countries the stamps are from. And sometimes
we wonder if we'll ever travel to some of the
countries whose stamps we like best: Great Britain
and Togo are two of my favorites.

*

My first letters actually written by me to my parents
were written in January 1964. Prior to that my
letters had been dictated to teachers or school staff
members.

*

Powerful writing
        Anyone who writes can unleash
Stories, hopes & fears

*

Racine Wis. January 19, 1964: Dear Mother and Daddy, Will you please send me a squirt gun? (No! Please) I did not like the Wizard of Oz. Flying monkeys are scary. Love and kisses Bill Mc

*

[Looking back, I have a strong memory of watching *The Wizard of Oz*. When the Wicked Witch of the West cackled to the flying monkeys, "Bring me Dorothy and her little dog, too," it was more than I could handle. I went into my bedroom—that happened to be right behind the television set—and listened to the movie; not that I had much choice. But just listening the story was not frightening at all and a few minutes later I went back out and rejoined the rest of the students to watch, if not enjoy, the rest of the movie.]

*

Ding dong such a witch
        Flying evil … monkeys
Toto scared like little me

*

Racine, Wis. Jan. 26, 1964: Dear Mother and
Daddy, I am wearing my Cub Scout uniform today.
I am sending you two of my best work papers. I
played "Monopoly" on Sunday. I did not watch
Lassie. It is 27 today. Love and kisses Bill Mc

*

Writing letters home
        Telling about my days & friends
Dreams: warm summer fun

*

January 29, 1964: My grandfather, Paw Paw, visited
today. Like daddy, he's an attorney. They work
together. He came and had lunch with me at the
school. I showed him around. He brought a
basketball signed by the coach and members of the
UK team. Later, after Paw Paw left, my friends and
I played basketball in the gym. Paw Paw is not very
tall but even if I grow taller than him, I'll always
look up to him.

*

February 9, 1964: We saw the Beatles tonight on Ed
Sullivan. They are a good band. Later, I listened to
some of their records. I like them a lot. But their
hair is funny. And they talk funny, too.

*

What is gray and blue and very big?
An elephant holding its breath.

*

February 17, 1964: For Christmas, along with the stamp album, I got an orange bag of all kinds of stamps. And there among all those stamps was one of an upside down biplane. It was a pretty cool stamp. But when Steve offered me, I'm not sure, eight or ten stamps for that one I felt pretty good about the trade.

*

[Steve, Joe, and I were roommates with David. For
some reason David went to bed when everyone else
did and we three got to stay up an hour later. We
would play games or read, or listen to records. I
liked records a lot; still do. I liked the Beatles,
Peter, Paul, and Mary, and Burl Ives and more. But
I liked "The Name Game," a lot. "Shirley burly mo
merly . . . Shirley." I bet I'll still be singing that
song when I'm old, maybe when I'm 64.]

*

Beatles aren't always bugs
      Sometimes they are bands
I like beetle bugs

*

Racine, Wis. March 17, 1964: Dear Mother and Daddy, What happened to my top and deck of cards? We had Indian Day on Saturday. Did you know Indians shoot arrows? Will you please send me an arrow kite. We flew kites on Sunday. But it was not a arrow kite. Love and kisses Bill

*

[Joe owned a shortwave radio which he brought upstairs with him one night. While David and the others slept, Joe, Steve and I would go up to the second floor classrooms. On this particular night, Joe showed us his radio. He turned it on, fiddled with the dials a bit, and magically we heard the voices of stars of *McHale's Navy* coming out of the radio: indeed the distinct voices of Ernest Borgnine, Tim Conway, and Joe Flynn filled the room. It wasn't the same as seeing the show—which we watched sometimes—but it was so cool, so much fun to listen to the show, one we knew well enough that we could 'see' what that night we could only hear. But that was the only night he pulled in a television show. On the other occasions he brought out the radio we listened to Green Bay Packers football games or, during baseball season, the Chicago Cubs games. Yet, more often than not, we'd play "Monopoly" or "Hi Ho Cherry-O," or "Game of the States" with Joe's radio sometimes keeping us company.]

*

Games of strategy and chance
      "Monopoly" and "Civil War"
No real violence

*

March 23, 1964: MOTOR PROGRAM When the children came back from Christmas vacation it is interesting to note that, if anything, three of our pupils had improved—Rick, Dougie and Bill McCann ad Bill was especially happy. Mike was again afraid of the "swinging bag," could not skip, and first day back on the program he was a very distressed little boy. However, it did not take many class sessions and he was back where he was before Christmas. Dougie and Rick can now bounce the ball, put one leg over it and then catch it, which is quite an accomplishment. Jumping rope is coming along nicely. In individual rope work Dougie can turn it twice and step over it, Rick can sometimes, and Bill McCann can almost do it twice—difficult to keep the arms swinging and the feet jumping, too. Basketball practice—dribbling, shooting at the basket—was coming good until the hole in the plaster stopped our practice. All four were getting pretty good at this. We're doing a little rhythm work this semester, using the sticks, then running, skipping, or marching in time. Bill McCann is best in this area; Rick could do better if he wasn't trying to make an "impression," and Dougie becomes uneasy if we continue for any length of time at this. Mike was ill when we started working with music and so has missed out on it. We've been working quite a bit on eye-control and eye-hand coordination, shooting at a target, shooting at the "bull's eye" on the blackboard. All like to do this, Rick and Dougie do the best; Bill next (He will shoot above the target at times) and Mike last. Mike is apt to shoot before he aims at the target unless cautioned, and then he is oftentimes high above the target. I have a small red ball and of a string swinging from the end of a stick and I swing this ball slowly back and forth in front of each child. They must not turn their heads but follow it with their eyes then when I say "hit" with their pointer finger coming from eye, shoulder, or hip position, they try to touch the moving ball—they're all getting it. Dougie is the quickest. Practice continues on the planks, balance board, jumping the swinging bag, skipping, hopping, galloping, etc. We've been enjoying this motor program time and hope that the results of our efforts will contribute to the pupils' success and days to come.

Edith De Moulpied

*

March 23, 1964: <u>Arithmetic</u> Bill is still working on the addition and subtraction combinations of numbers 1-10. He still needs help of some kind on many combinations. I believe some of his difficulty is because of the pressure he feels from the older children. <u>Writing</u> Bill knows all the cursive hand and manuscript lower case letters. I believe he knows some of the upper case. He learned very quickly how to transpose manuscript to cursive. His writing is skillfully done. Writing is getting easier for him and he does not require so much time to get his work done. Bill is very conscientious in doing his work. He is steady but rather slow to finish most of his work. He gets quite perturbed when he is right in the middle of some piece of work and is called to get ready for his exercises. Hardly a day goes by when he doesn't complain about having to leave his work unfinished. Especially in a group activity he joins in with the foolish talk and actions of Billy O. When I talk to these two boys about this Bill acts quite offended by it. He tries to excuse himself [by] putting all the blame on Billy O. It takes awhile for him to discard his hurt feelings. Generally speaking, enjoy having Bill in my classroom.

Mrs. Schwager

*

March 23, 1964: Observations. Bill's attitude is very good. When we settled down to really [do] spelling his comment was: "I like it. Let's have spelling every day." Bill is observing. I removed 11 and 12 from a work book we were using in a group activity—didn't say anything about it. Bill was the only one in the group who noticed, and he was very distressed saying: "What's the matter with my book? Eleven always comes after ten. Something's wrong here." Bill likes to finish whatever he starts and takes pride in his work. He has come a long way from the little boy who was quite a problem and who had a s a favorite expression: "I can't do this. Help me."

Edith De Moulpied

*

March 25, 1964: Dear Mr. and Mrs. McCann: Attached is the sales slip for the shoes we purchased for Bill. Kindly make your check payable to The Cove Schools. Thank you. Sincerely yours, (Mrs.) Marie Mikulecky, Secretary

*

Racine Wis. April 2, 1964: Dear Mother and Daddy, thank you for the candy, toys, cards and a painting set. Tuesday we watched some men cut down trees. They made a lot of noise. Later they made a big pile of wood that some of the boys played on until they were made to stop. Love and kisses Bill

[Sometimes my letters home make no sense without a little research. It turns out that Easter was March 29, 1964. And Passover was March 27 through April 4, 1964. These were important dates that year because, though exact numbers changed constantly, the school's student population of 24 was generally divided among those who were Catholic, Jewish, and Protestant.

[No one held themselves out as being agnostic or atheist. No one had a more exotic belief, though had they, it would have been accommodated. Weekly, Catholic students went to Mass—though not on the school grounds—and fish was served every Friday. Jewish students went to synagogue and Hebrew School and during Passover matzo was served in the dining room instead of bread.

[For we Protestants, there was Sunday School, taught at the Cove on Sunday mornings. During Advent an Advent Calendar was hung up in the hallway where we assembled before going into meals and where Advent presents were taken from the numbered spots each day and hung on the felt Christmas tree at the top of the calendar. Still, in the early 1960s these were the accommodations that passed for actions of diversity and inclusion.

[I say this not to be dismissive but to recognize that these were indeed significant accommodations at that point in time: WWII was only 'yesterday's news' and not yet 'history;' Catholics were discriminated against socially, educationally, and sometimes in other ways as well. At the age of eight I didn't care about such things, but presumably the parents of students might have cared. The Strausses were Jewish, having escaped from Germany via Spain prior to 1937, the year they immigrated to the United States. But for practical reasons—the need for a school that could help their child being first and foremost; the fact that the Cove Schools was a unique institution, the only one of its kind in the country, best I can tell—it might well be parents put aside any 'discomfort' "for the sake of the children." So, in the context of 1964 my letter of April 2, 1964, was for the purpose of thanking my parents for the Easter presents that they'd sent me. After all, my birthday was not until May 8, when I'd turn nine!]

*

April 10, 1964: The Cove Schools, Racine "$8.95 paid.

*

June 5, 1964: Bill McCann Bill is a good student and accepts his assignments eagerly, then he does them neatly and carefully. He stays in his seat, raises his hand if he has a question or is finished with his work. Once in awhile he comes out with a remark or answer that sounds a little "smart alecky" but he is sensitive and immediately realizes what he has said and why I don't approve—or he sometimes wants an explanation and I try to make it clear to him. If there is an errand to be done I can count on Bill to do it for me. It is a pleasure to have him in the class room.

Edith De Moulpied

*

June 27, 1964: Mom thinks I can swim. I'm not so sure. It's a long way across the pool.

*

July 3, 1964: We went crabbing today. Crabs are delicious. Tomorrow we are going deep sea fishing. I can't wait. I wonder if we go way out, like to England, or maybe just to Cape Canaveral.

*

July 15, 1964: While the family was at the beach someone moved all our stuff from the house in town to our new house in the country. It's a big house. I even have my own bedroom. Mom and Dad still have to share a bedroom.

*

We live on a farm
        Neighbors aren't next door
No mean blood! Fresh air!

*

September 25, 1964: Ephraim Roseman, M.D. Louisville, KY Re: Bill McCann Dear Mrs. Strauss The father of Bill McCann has asked me to write you concerning his medication, According to our schedule he is discontinuing all medicine. I am delighted about this and I am sure you will be. If you have any questions please let me know. Sincerely,   (signed) E. Roseman, M.D.

*

Racine Wis. Oct 13, 1964: Dear Mother and Daddy,
How is the dog? How is Laura doing in school? It is
going to be warmer today. We watched "Flipper"
on Saturday. Love and kisses
Bill M.

*

Racine Wis. Oct 27,1964: Dear Mother and Daddy,
How is Bruce after his birthday? Did he get my
card? It is cloudy today. How is Laura doing in
school? We have a new boy in our classroom and a
new girl. They have names I can't spell. I am
sending home a good work paper. Thank you for the
package. Love and kisses Bill M.

*

How do you shoot a blue elephant?
    With a blue elephant gun!

*

Racine, Wis. Nov. 17, 1964: Dear Mother and
Daddy Would you please send me a talking puppet?
What did Susan get for her birthday? It is 44° here
now. A boy here got a toy named "Mr. Machine."
Wind it up and it walks. Ring its bell, too. I like
doing that. It's a fun toy. And the boy is fun to play
with to.

*

Oh, joys of fall call:
        Birthdays, yes! & Halloween
Best season? Of course!

*

December 11, 1964: Academic Report Bill McCann
There is real competition between Billy O and Bill
Mc in arithmetic. Once and awhile it gets too much
for Bill and he breaks down. His spare time is spent
working puzzles or on some project of his.

Mrs. Schwager

*

December 1964: BILL MCCANN MOTOR
DEVELOPMENT PROGRAM Bill McCann
cooperates well, He's a little on the slow side—little
awkward and needs to "limber up." He needs more
catching and throwing practice. His timing for
running and in and out when jumping rope is
showing improvement. He is now able to bounce
the ball and get his leg over—sometimes several
times, and he is starting to turn his own rope.
Balancing on the balance board is improving. He
can count and clap his hands in time but has trouble
getting his feet to go right. He is always coming up
with ideas of things that we can do and some of his
ideas are good. I think the thing we must do with
Bill is to get him to move a "smoother" and easier.

*

[The critiques and insights of December 1964 are
valid today. I still walk a crooked mile. If I were
asked to pass a field sobriety test, I couldn't.
Impossible.]

Pretty Christmas tree
    Tiny ornaments adorn
Not all will adore

*

Circa 1964, with Dad, Laura, and Bruce.
    (Photograph by Mom)

1965: Joe Goes Home

Jan 17, 1965: Dear Mom and Dad, How are you doing? I am fine. Have you had any snow yet? We have snow. Lots of snow. Out behind the kitchen some of the boys made a slide for the sleds to go down it was fun to make. Jamie and Seth and some boys and girls made a snow fort. Later, I joined in the snowball fight. I am having fun. But I hope spring comes soon. Winter is cold. Love Bill Mc

*

[Usually we played on the lake side of the Cove's building. If not there, we'd walk further away from the building altogether to where there was a pretty good hill we could sled down. My memory of the occasion when the slide was made was that it was after dinner. Usually, after dinner we might walk around the building—a distance equal to about three blocks, I'd guess—but for whatever reason we were guided to the back of the building, not far from the kitchen and there cooperatively a bunch of us built a ramp, I'm guessing this far after the event that was maybe 4 feet tall and maybe 4 feet wide by five or six feet long. For reference, nine-year-old me probably wasn't four feet tall; certainly not much beyond that, if at all. So, we felt like this was a pretty big deal.

[Looking back, my memory was that we used metal saucers to sled down our 'slide' and not sleds. But I do remember that it was a fun time. We were working together for a common goal. The next day, as I recall, Jamie and Seth made the 'fort' which was a kind of half circular wall made of large rolled-snowballs with snow stuffed in any holes to create a solid wall no more than maybe six feet long (because it was next to a large tree), just across the driveway from the fire escape that was outside what had been my room back in spring 1962 (and would be in the 65-66 school year). After they'd built their fort—and stockpiled some snowballs behind it—Steve and Joe and me and some others were hit with flying snowballs, so we fought back. It was lots of fun.]

*

How do you shoot a red elephant?
        Choke it till it turns blue, then shoot it with a blue elephant gun.

*

Racine, Wis February 23, 1965: Dear Mother and Daddy, I do not like Sam and I do not like girls. I was in bed on Sonday. It is 14° today. It is snowing here today. Will you please send me a different book on art? I have 11 work books. I lost one of my teeth. Will the Tooth Fairy visit me in Racine? Love and kisses Bill Mc

*

Yesterday's spelling word
          Sonday—Jesus' day instead of
Sunday—movies day

*

March 26, 1965: Bill McCann Academic Report
<u>Reading</u> Bill is reading on an early third grade level. He uses the phonetic approach to new vocabulary. Many times he is able to pick out familiar parts of the word and then the rest of the word is easy. Bill's oral reading fluency improved so much since Christmas. He loves to read and much of his spare time is spent in reading Reader's Digest books. Bill has excellent comprehension. Most of his seatwork is from third grade workbooks. <u>Arithmetic</u> Since Christmas Bill has learned to carry when adding two place numbers, and to borrow when subtracting two place numbers. It usually takes him longer to grasp a new step in arithmetic but when he gets it he usually retains it. <u>Writing</u> Bill knows and uses both cursive and manuscript lower and upper case letters. His writing is. skillfully and neatly done. Bill has ambition and determination to get ahead. None of his spare time is wasted. Besides doing a great deal of reading he has become interested in studying about different animals or fish. This he finds in the dictionary.

Mrs. Schwager

*

[The school only had four teachers. But it did have some adjunct faculty—though those 'faculty' were fully unaware of their status. Walter Cronkite and Jules Bergman were the most reliable and, even today, the best known. Other occasional such faculty included Captain Kangaroo, Mr. Green Jeans, and Walt Disney. Walt was pretty much a weekly presence as he introduced the segments of his show and talked about the wonders of his future Florida theme park with its hosts, Mickey and Minnie Mouse and its theme parks that were to include Tomorrowland. But at six and seven, even 10 and 11 such an idea seemed too far off to take seriously. Meanwhile, Captain Kangaroo visited only when a child was sick, and even then only on weekdays.

[But Cronkite and Bergman often seemed to be everywhere, all the time. Whenever a Gemini rocket went up or came down, Jules Bergman was always there to answer Walter Cronkite's questions or to make an astute observation. And Walter Cronkite? Well, even as a young child, it seemed to me that he was everywhere, all-knowing, if not all-powerful. He was on the evening news, declaiming and explaining events of the day. He was present for every liftoff and splashdown, accompanied by Jules Bergman who understood how rockets were fueled, how spacemen were trained and strapped into their tiny capsules; he seemed to know everything about space and science and . . . well, just about everything.

[Walter Cronkite made sense of the world to us. Even if the events did not make sense to him, Cronkite made meaning of the death of a president, as he narrated and explained the ceremonies and pageantry surrounding it to his youngest viewers in Racine. Indeed, even now I still remember feeling rather certain that if I had access to Jules Bergman and a couple of Walts—Cronkite and Disney—and maybe a *World Book Encyclopedia* that it might be possible to know (or at least find out) everything there was to know about the world outside the Cove Schools of Racine, WI.]

*

Racine, Wis April 13, 1965: Dear Mother and
Daddy, We are having an Easter Party today. We
hunted for eggs. We also ate cookies that looked
like eggs. They had frosting on them that tasted
good. Are you having an Easter party? I had a good
time with you. I enjoyed going to the zoo and
looking for sea glass, too. How are you feeling
mother? Love and kisses Bill Mc

*

[Easter and Halloween were the holidays (and
birthdays, of course) celebrated at the Cove. The
Easter party was held on the third floor in the gym
which always seemed ginormous, with a really tall
ceiling. Anyway, the focus of the party was a very
large papier mâché and chicken wire chicken that
was probably 10 feet long, four feet wide, probably
4 ½ feet tall at the bottom of its yellow beak and 5
feet tall at the top of its head with a red comb above
that. It was monstrous!

[Painted red and yellow with white highlights that
rooster was (and still is to my way of thinking) one
of the coolest sculptures I've ever seen. Seated on a
large piece of canvas (used to help move it easily)
covered in straw and in which candies and Easter
eggs were hidden, it was at the heart of our Easter
celebrations. So of course, this was where our
Easter egg hunt was held. Indeed it was a setting in
which every child could succeed. These were really
fun events—as evidenced by the fact that I still
remember them 60 years later.]

Racine Wis. April 20, 1965: Dear Mother and Daddy, Did you get Laura's school work yet? A new girl is coming today. We had two rabbits on the third floor for the Easter party. One of them is all white. The other is white and black. They are in one of the alcoves so we have to go over there to pet them. But that's okay. It's still fun to pet the rabbits. Love and kisses Bill Mc

*

[The gym was on the third floor. At one end of the gym was a large storage area—where the chicken was kept, along with tricycles and two-wheeled scooters, holiday decorations, a large number of over-sized cardboard blocks painted red and white, and other stuff—there was a standup piano usually someplace up there (where we not only had gym but music and parties and events such as A Day in Town) and two windowed alcoves. There were some built-in storage closets in the alcoves. And it was in one of the alcoves that the rabbits (one black and white, one totally white) were kept for about a week, as I recall. Anyway, Steve, Joe and I would go up there during that week to play with the rabbits. When we got bored with the rabbits we'd go get a few of the cardboard bricks to block off the alcove's opening and play marbles in the other alcove.]

*

Racine Wis May 5, 1965: Dear Mother and Daddy, How is Paw Paw feeling? It is cloudy today. The temperature is 42° here this morning. I am learning multiplication. We went by bus to the Museum of Science and Industry last Thursday. I love going there. It is one of my favorite places. We saw dinosaurs. They were huge. Steve said birds are dinosaurs, too. Is that true? Love and kisses Bill

*

[I'm not certain but I remember one of my birthday celebrations at the Cove and I think it was the one in 1965: we children were all assembled in the 'great room,' a large space with several tables, a large (probably 26" screen) television that at the top was probably five feet off the ground and lots of chairs, enough for all of us with extras for the adults. Anyway, I remember a large, tall box, with quite a few toys in it. I don't remember most of the toys; the one that caught my imagination, though, looked like a finger and was called—"Six Finger." It was a toy gun that you could hold between the four fingers of one hand and then use the thumb to shoot the dart that could be put in the end of the pink plastic finger. Another toy—probably at the suggestion of Mrs. Strauss—was a model of "The Visible Man."]

*

May 17, 1965: Racine, Wis. Dear Mother and
Daddy, What day am I going home? I miss the
farm. We had movies on Sunday. °The temperature
is about 48°. It is getting warmer. How are the
puppies doing? We went by bus to Petrifying
Springs for a picnic. How are you? Love and kisses
Bill Mc

*

On that picnic a friend (Joe, probably) and I agreed
to see who could eat the most wild onions. I ate
100+. Boy, even today I remember being sick
afterwards, until no lunch remained.

*

Wild onions eaten
        are best in smaller servings
not batches of 100

Spring 1965: Dr. Marie Strauss likely took this family photo

Racine, Wis. June 1, 1965: Dear Mother and Daddy, Mr. Olson and Mrs. Schwager were not here so we went to the beach and looked for rocks and some pieces of glass. How are Laura and Bruce doing in schools? I can't wait to come home. It is starting to feel like summer. The temperature is 65° here today. What has Daddy been doing on the farm lately? Are there strawberries yet? How about grapes? How are the 7 calves doing? Love and kisses Bill Mc

*

June 5, 1965: Joe came to tell me that his parents had come to pick him up. He was going home for the summer. But he wasn't coming back in the fall. Instead, he'd be attending school in his hometown of Appleton, Wisconsin. We looked at each other. But I don't think either of us knew what to do. I don't know about Joe, but I remember wanting to hug him. Instead, after a few more awkward moments, like adults, we shook hands. And then he turned and ran out of our shared room, happy to be heading home.

*

Alone after Joe left
        knew not what to feel or do
joyless loneliness

*

June 1965: Bill McCann Academic Report <u>Reading</u> Bill is reading on a fourth grade level. He is a fluent reader and has excellent comprehension. <u>Arithmetic</u> Since the Easter report Bill has learned to multiply two-place numbers by 2 and 3 with carrying and without. <u>Spelling</u> Bill's spelling is on a latter third grade level. His attack on words is by auditory memory. There has been a big improvement in his spelling since learning the vowel sounds and a few spelling rules. He needs little help with spelling when writing his letter to his parents. Bill's even temperament, politeness, and cooperation have all helped to make this a successful year for him. Bill matured this year and socially outgrew the other children. They admired Bill and looked up to him much the same as the children did to Joseph in Mr. Olson's room. I shall miss him in my room next fall.

Mrs. Schwager

*

Postcard of Empire State Building New York City
(front) July 2, 1965 Dear Mrs Strauss We are in
New York City We have seen the Words Fair and
Empire State Building Love Bill Mc

*

Broadway in New York
          Plays, music & dance every night
Great way to spend days.

*

[That was my first trip to New York. Laura and I,
Mom and Dad went to New York to stay with Aunt
Pam, who was trying to become a success as an
actress, while attending the World's Fair. When the
sitcom *That Girl!* starring Marlo Thomas came on, I
always imagined that that was the life that Aunt
Pam was living. But like *That Girl*, Pam had little
success, a single short film, no Broadway or Off-
Broadway credits, and a national Dove commercial.
Still, when she was trying to become the first to fly
across the Atlantic in an open gondola balloon, Pam
was on Johnny Carson. But in 1965 all of that was
ahead.

[Instead, Aunt Pam lived in a tall apartment
building and while I don't remember the building, I
do remember the terror I felt when Laura and I went
to run an errand of some sort or other and neither of
us could remember the door that Pam's apartment
was behind! I think we'd only gone up or down a

floor, so we got back to the right floor—but all the doors looked just alike. Obviously, we were found, or we found the right apartment—but that was a scary time. In addition to seeing the Fair, we also saw a Broadway play—Joel Gray in *How to Succeed in Business Without Really Trying*. Today, I'm a playwright, a member of the Dramatists Guild, hoping to have my own Broadway success by really trying.]

*

Laura & I lost
         only one floor gone down (or up)
Terror: no parent around

*

July 14, 1965: Dear Bill It is very thoughtful and kind of you to send me greetings from New York. You know last Christmas I was in New York when the Fair was closed, but I went to the United Nations Building. Mrs. Mikulecky is writing this on the typewrite so you can read it yourself; my handwriting is hard to read. It's awfully hot and humid today, but here in the office at school it is alright. There are stamps from Jamaica enclosed in this letter. Are you still collecting stamps? Give my very best regards to your family and to you, Bill, my big boy, a hug and good wishes for a happy time at home from your friend, Mrs. Strauss.

*

[Mrs. Strauss was the administrative head of the school. Frankly, even now I don't know what that means. To me, she was the person who was a grandmother away from home. She told me that she, like her husband, was a doctor. But I don't know what kind. Instead, I knew her to be kind. Though she was the 'boss'—or that was how I thought of her—she was the person who took kids shopping for shoes, or trousers, or whatever clothes we needed, instead of giving the task to someone else. But most of all I remember her as patient, kind, and a wonderful grandmother to every child there at 'her' school. (Which is how I thought of it. Certainly, that was not an idea that she ever expressed.)]

*

August 14, 1965: I can swim! I made it all the way across the pool without stopping. Now Laura and I can both go in the deep end! Dad can teach me to body surf!

*

September 14, 1965: Good to see Steve again. He's one smart guy with lots of interests. He collects stamps, seems to know everything about the weather and science, and he plays chess. We often play cribbage in the mornings before breakfast. He's taught me how to play chess but I'm not very good. Maybe I'll get better. I don't think I know anyone our age who is smarter than Steve.

*

Joe's not back
        Living in Appleton
See you soon, Joe?

*

October 4, 1965: Dear Mother and Dad, How are you doing on the farm? Friday we played games and then some boys and I dug a hole. We wanted to play "Combat!" Saturday we dug a second hole and also played with guns. We also flew a kite. Sunday we played kickballs I got a letter from Aunt Boo. Will we see her when we go to the beach? We had coke and cookies for treat. Love Bill

*

October 20, 1965: Mr. Olson is a pretty cool teacher. He does things differently than my other teachers. We play "Battleship" on graph paper. And we watch programs on television some, too. We watch Gemini launches, and also the splashdowns.

*

Monday November 1, 1965: Dear Mom and Dad How are you doing? I am fine. We watched Walt Disney. We had a Halloween party on the third floor. I was Zoro. It was like a carnival we had candy and witches brew and also cookies. Later, we went Trick or Treating around the school building. I was Zoro then too. Love Bill Mc

*

Nov. 9, 1965: Dear Mom and Dad, We started Cub scouts on Monday. There are five of us in a den. We all have a job to do after School. Steven takes care of the coats. Tom takes care of the Mittens Peter takes care of the scarps. Jamie takes care of the weather and I take care of the chairs. We went to Memorial Hall on Sunday afternoon at 2:15 and got back about 4 o'clock that afternoon. We saw some stamps. We got some French cookies and we got some Italian cookies too. We ate the Italian cookies at Memorial Hall. We brought back some French cookies for treat. We also had movies. Love Bill Mc

*

Cub Scout uniform
        of gold and blue inspires a
good turn daily, too.

*

Cub Scout, Summer 1966

December 4, 1965: Mr. Olson let us watch the launch of Gemini 4 today from Cape Kennedy in Florida. It is so much fun to find out about space flight from people on television. And then the rocket fires up and moments later it's like the rocket was never on the ground at all. First it becomes a speck on the T.V. screen and then it's . . . gone.

*

December 7, 1965: Dear Mom and Dad Friday a group watched Family Classics and also a group played games. Saturday morning we went outside. Some of the boys made forts in the bushes. Saturday we played outside till time for treat. Saturday night a group watched *Flipper*, Sunday morning we went to Sunday school and we also went outside. Sunday afternoon we watched *Rudolph the Red Nosed Reindeer*. We also had movies. They were about the American Cowboy and Snowyday. I am making Santa's work shop in art. How are you doing? I am fine. It is a very sunny day today. We planted some North Dakota Hard Red spring wheat and some North Dakota Durum. We planted the wheat on 12/1/65. Love Bill Mc

*

Recreation Report Bill McCann December 10, 1965: Bill is very mature and responsible and frequently had his own ideas and projects with which he likes to work. He prefers more advanced table games, such as monopoly and civil war. Bill seems to like team games and would probably be more enthused about organized games if there were children of his interest and skill level. Bill enjoys working on projects in the art room, and particularly enjoys working with wood. Working on his stamp collection and cub scout projects are favorite activities.

(signed) Sharon Johns

*

Class grown Durum wheat
      May grow very tall and wave
But it will not bake

*

Bill McCann December 1965: <u>General Behavior</u>: His work habits are excellent. He cheerfully accepts the work, sticks to the task until it is finished and then, if anything is wrong, he will gladly re-o it until it is correct. One thing I have noticed, Bill does things the way he is taught to do them. There is little room for any other way, He can be trusted to do on his own. He seems to accept correction fairly well, His spare time is utilized in constructive activity of some sort. He will read one of his magazines or a library book or an encyclopedia. He is stimulated by Steve's ability and interest in science. Bill's relations with the other children is good. He makes friends easily. Perhaps a part of this is that he is "business" like and does what he is told to do. He does not create a disturbance. This attribute is an asset for any future job and should be a commending factor in any recommendation.

Bill, at times, is rather outspoken and does expound upon the weakness of others. One day he said something to Jim about one glaring fault. Jim grumbled something about, "Boy, you sure know how to hurt a guy." Most of the children in the room are attracted to him. In Bill's "book" Jim is the "odd-man" out. Part of this is directly related to Jim's silliness and teasing. Bill does not usually shift "emotional gears" easily. If he is serious, his mood does not change to silliness quickly. Bill could be termed a leader in our group, at least part of the time. He comes up with good and interesting ideas from his magazine and from other sources.

<u>Reading:</u> Bill likes to read things having to do with adventure. He is reading material on about a 4th grade level. He does hold the concepts of the material. He seems to be able to link them with other information he possesses. Currently, we are reading "Pioneer Pilgrim". It holds a great deal of interest for him. He is easily stimulated to look to related subjects and report on them, wither verbally or in short written reports. Bill has a great interest in library books. He has read at least eight that I know of.

<u>Spelling:</u> Bill's approach to spelling is fairly sound. He uses a dictionary when he needs help or he will ask for it. If I give him the individual sounds of a word he can sound it out. If the word is not phonetic and I give him the spelling I must go slow and give him only a couple letters at a time. He doesn't seem to be able to more than this at one time. I believe he is able to but lacks the training.

<u>Arithmetic:</u> I've noticed Bill is dependent on some forms of counting for figuring out addition and subtraction problems. He uses the abacus at times and at other times I've observed him utilizing a tally system. He seems to have the process of carrying and borrowing down. He works slowly. We are currently working on multiplying two and three place numbers by 2,3,4, and 5. Bill's story problem 'sense' is showing some potential in simple situations, again, he is somewhat slow.

Herbert J. Olson

1966: On the Launch Pad

My mother's father, John Y. Brown, Sr. (Paw Paw) circa 1980, a photo of a portion of an original oil on board portrait. Photo editing by author, who owns the original portrait.

[On January 7, 1966 I went to work with Paw Paw. He was a member of the General Assembly in Frankfort, the Majority Floor Leader of the House of Representatives. He actually got me a job as a page. So when he went on the floor, I got to go with him. When we got there a man at the door to the chamber opened it and greeted him, "Good Morning, Brown." "Good Morning, this is my grandson, Bill. He's going to be a page today." "Nice to meet you, Bill," the man replied. "Nice to meet you, too," I said before hurrying after Paw Paw who was still walking down the center aisle.

[He stopped in front of a large wedding cake-like bunch of desks. "That's the Speaker's dais," said my grandfather. I didn't say anything. I didn't know what either a speaker or a dais was, but I was too busy taking everything in to ask questions. "Now, Bill" he said. "take one of these seats facing the Speaker." I did as he'd said. The chairs had their backs to the large roll-top desks that filled most of the space in the room. The chairs were big, covered in brown leather, and quite comfortable. I kind of sank into the seat a bit.

["Do you see that big board up there with names and green and red light bulbs, numbers, and names?" "Yes, sir." "Those names are last names of the members of House, here. Beside each name is a number and a green and red light bulb. Each member votes on legislation by using a switch on their desk. Green is for 'Yes.' Red is for 'No.' Each of the members has a desk and each desk a number. So if you see a light go on next to a number, go find the desk that has the same number and ask the member what you can do for him. Some may want you to go get a bill from the Bill Room in the basement, others may want something from the snack bar. Those are the most likely errands you'll be asked to run. Do you remember coming past the snack bar and the Bill Room?" "Yes, sir." "Ok. Good." And then my grandfather was gone.

[I didn't see him anywhere. A light on the board went on and a child about my age, I was 10, got up out of his chair and went to see how he could be helpful. A few minutes later another light went on and I looked around. No one else seemed to notice the light. So I guessed it must be my turn. I looked at the board again—to make sure I knew what the desk number was. It was only a couple of rows back of where I was sitting, so I went to the desk and asked the man sitting there, "What can I do for you, sir?" "Here's some change. Would you please go to the snack bar and bring me back a Coca-Cola, please?" "Yes, sir," I said, hurrying toward the elevator and never thinking to see where Paw Paw might be, or to check in with him.

[I went to the elevator we'd come up on maybe ten minutes before, and waited. When the door opened, after those who were on it got off, I and others got on and I rode down to the basement. When the door opened in the basement I got off. I looked around just a bit and then noticed the crowd coming towards me, several people had newspapers or soft drink bottles. So it didn't take much to figure out exactly where the Snack Bar was. Once there, I had found a Coke and was making my way toward the cash register when I heard my grandfather call out to me, "What are you doing, Bill? We need to leave." "Someone asked me to bring him a Coke." "Oh. Ok. Well, I'll wait here. Hurry back, so we can leave."

[So I delivered the Coke and came back a few minutes later to find Paw Paw in conversation with someone. After he was finished, we left. And eventually, I got a check for $6.00 for serving as a Page. That was my first job.]

*

I worked my first
     job, a page in Frankfort
is that my future?

January 24, 1966: Dear Mom and Dad, We are studying about South America. If you can find any articles or maps in the paper? Could you please send them in your letter? Do you think I could have a battery for my radio? If I can, would you please send one! I am beginning to learn to play chess. I hope I can get to play it soon. Friday a group of us watched *Peter Pan & Family Classics*. Steve and Mr. Lowry played chess. I played a game too. Saturday, I worked on my chuck wagon. I am working on Division. It's fun. I am also finishing up a good book called *Pioneer Pilgrim*. Call soon! Love Bill

*

February 1, 1966: Dear Mom and Dad, How are you doing? I am fine. Is Susan feeling better? How is Bruce doing in writing letters now? Friday a group watched *Family classics*. Saturday was theme day, I was superman. We made the costumes in the morning and we played games in the afternoon. A group watched "*I dream of Jeanie* and *Flipper* on Saturday night. Sunday we had Sunday School and in the afternoon we had movies. One of the movies was about hamsters. They were good movies. Sunday night a group watched Walt Disney and *Lassie*. Call soon! Love, Bill

*

Wanting to know how my
        Siblings are doing
curiosity or loneliness?

*

February 22, 1966: Mrs. McCann: Some of Bill's slacks are too small. In regard to correct size it would be advantageous for us to buy them here, but if you prefer to purchase them there, Bill's waist is 30-32. Best regards Marie C. Strauss

*

March 1, 1966: Dear Mom and Dad, How are you doing? I am fine. Friday, after treat we went outside and played til about 4:00 in the afternoon. Then we went inside and the bigger boys stayed down to get their baths. Matt, John, Dave stayed down to get their baths too because they get their baths with the big boys. After dinner the other boys had baths. Then a group watched TV. They watched *Rocky and his Friends*. After *Rocky and his Friend*s they watched *Family Classics*. It was about Moby Dick. Next week is about the Lone Ranger. Saturday was Philippine Island Day. In the morning we made mats to sit on. In the morning a group went up on the third floor to learn a Philippine dance and that afternoon some people came and danced for us. That afternoon we sat on the mats we had made that morning. After the dance we had some slides. They were on the Philippine Islands. They were good. After the slides we went downstairs and went outside. After we came in it was time for treat. We had coconut Hawaiian punch and Jamie's cookies. After dinner we watched TV. We watched *Flipper* and *I Dream of Jeanie*. Sunday we had movies before treat. I did not see them because I was out with the Clarks. We had Sunday School. Love Bill Mc

*

[Leila Clark was my mom's closest friend when they were children, living only a few blocks apart. Later they went to high school and then to the University of Kentucky together. So I guess it must have seemed natural for Leila and her husband, Bill, to treat me like family and take me out on the weekends some, especially since they lived in the Chicago area and Bill worked as an editor in downtown Chicago. I know that they once took me to Billy Mitchell Field in Milwaukee to have lunch and watch the planes land and take off. One weekend I spent with them at their home when their daughter Leslie was still a toddler. But the event I remember best was the time they were taking me to spend the weekend with them and I read aloud every sign from the Cove School's gate until we walked into their house! I must have driven them nuts. But I was so proud of my ability to read. I wanted to show off, to share my newfound ability with them.]

*

Airplanes come and go
     People of every shape & size
Crowd our friendly skies

*

[Mr. Olson taught us in a more hands-on fashion than some of his colleagues; he was a bit more 'relaxed,' a little less regimented. He had us play "Battleship" on graph paper. All of us would play. Four students and Mr. Olson, too. We'd call out a location and a classmate's name and try to sink everyone's 'battleship.' There were no plastic pegs or roaring sounds or flashing lights. Just dual 10 x 10 grids drawn on paper with lines to indicate ships and x's to show "hits." And we had such fun!]

*

April 10, 1966: I was sooooo happy to be home for Easter. The Easter Bunny came, of course. Everyone got all dressed up. Looking so nice. We went to church. All of that was nice. But what I'd been so looking forward to was hunting for Easter Eggs out in the big side yard at Lammom's house in Winchester with all my McCann family cousins. I'd secretly been looking forward to being part of the scramble to see who could find the most eggs and jellybeans and such. My Aunt Carolyn—Dad's sister—was being nice, being kind, when she said to me, "Bill, you're a big boy now. Can you help me hide the eggs for the little kids to find?" I held a grudge against her for that for years. But it wasn't her fault. I didn't speak up. How could she know I had been looking forward to hunting for Easter eggs if I didn't tell her? Actually, I hadn't told anyone. Not my parents. Not Laura or Bruce.

*

April 26, 1966: Dear Mom and Dad Thank you for the pants and socks. How are you doing? I am fine. How is Daddy doing at the office? Have you started the Spring planting yet? Friday we watched "Snow Fire" on *Family Classics*. Friday afternoon after school I planted some watermelon seeds. I went to art Friday night. Saturday we had a Circus I was ring-master. We had a Snake Charmer. We also had an acrobat and some others. Sunday we had Sunday School. After rest period we went outside. We had treat during movies. We watched Walt Disney. Love, Bill

*

Mom and me, circa 1966
(Photograph by Dad taken at Racine, WI Zoo)

May 10, 1966: Dear Mom and Dad, How are you doing? I am fine. Last Thursday we went to the Milwaukee Zoo. We went by bus. I liked the birds and monkey's best. About 1:30 we were on our way back. Saturday we had a Cub Scout meeting in the morning. Saturday afternoon we had the Cub Scout ceremony. I became a Bear! Saturday night a group went to the art room. A group watched "I dream of Jeanie." It was good. Sunday we had Sunday School. It was about Jesus. It was good. I got a card from Lila & Bill. Thank you for the birthday gifts. Love, Bill

*

[I remember watching all the launches and splashdowns of the various space rockets that went up or came down during my time at the Cove Schools. And always Jules Bergman and Walter Cronkite were close at hand, explaining it all.]

*

June 6, 1966: Dear Mom and Dad, This morning we saw the splash down of Gemini 9 live from the USS Wasp. The astronauts are safe on the USS Wasp. The USS Wasp has picked up three other spaceships besides Gemini 9. They were all Geminis thou. It was interesting. Friday I wrote to the Navy. If you get anything for me from the US Navy please save it for me. Thank you. Friday night a group went to art. Saturday night, we had a cook-out. It was fun. We had chopsuie and coleslaw. It was good. Mrs. Johnson brought some books to Sunday School to read to us. Sunday night a group went to art. This week we are going to close the art room for the summer. Love Bill

*

Gemini rockets
    go up, come back down
out pop astronauts

*

March 28, 1966: WILLIAM MCCANN PSYCHOLOGICAL SUMMARY Bill is a child with mild brain damage who is making an excellent functional recovery. He now functions in the low average range when dealing with verbal materials and at a borderline retarded level when performance materials are used. Spatial organization and representation of form are now very acceptable for his age but the good results he attains are achieved by various compensatory means such as working slowly and carefully with continuous checking. Consequently he sometimes misses some aspects of the field through heavy concentration on others. Placement in a regular classroom may be successful at this time in view of the good attitude toward learning, the good reading skill and interest in new information. He will be pressured because of his slowness and need to work extra carefulness as well as the need for explicit instruction and frequent review. Many children with ability levels in the slow or dull-normal range feel more comfortable and are more successful if they are placed one year below age expectancy in order to equalize the competition with bright normal children somewhat, and such placement would be in order for Bill. A special education teacher who would be available on a daily basis during the school day to work with him individually is essential, with special adjustments of this nature for an indeterminate period of time it can be anticipated that Bill will continue to progress at a slower than average rate and eventually become fully able to take a place in society,   (signed)   Laura E, Lehtinen, Ph.D. Clinical Director

*

March 28, 1966 :

Bill is a child

in the low

average range

. Spatial organization and representation

are achieved by various compensatory means such as working slowly and carefully with continuous checking.

Placement in a regular classroom may be successful

Many children with ability levels in the slow   range feel more comfortable and are more successful if they are placed one year below age expectancy

such placement would be in order for Bill.
special

adjustments   can be anticipated   Bill will
progress at a slower than average rate
and eventually become fully able to take a place in
society,

>(signed)
>Laura E, Lehtinen, Ph.D.
>Clinical Director

*

Bill can become
    fully able to take a place
in society

Epilogue

[I received my Eagle Scout rank, Boy Scouts of
America in June 1973. In June 1975, I graduated
from Lafayette High School, Lexington, Kentucky,
in the top third of my class. And that fall I headed
off to college.]

*

Eagle Scout flying
        High school graduate walking
Head high, future ahead.

*

APPENDICES

Notes

1.   (page 25) Myoclonic Epilepsy: it is now believed that the proper diagnosis today would be Doose Syndrome.

2.   (page 27) The Cove Schools accepted children described as "educationally or mentally retarded," a term which covered a great deal of ground. At this time—roughly from 1959 to 1966—I am variously described in these documents as having had epileptic seizures; being mentally retarded; having problems with coordination, speaking, and walking; behavioral issues (including what is now called ADHD—Attention Deficit Hyperactivity Disorder) and having perceptual disabilities. So far as I am aware, students at the Cove Schools in Racine all had some combination of those issues. Today, there are far more types of problems that fall into the broad category of "special education." But what we now know as Special Education did not exist in Kentucky until 1975, and tracing the various name changes would require a book, not a paragraph in a poetry collection. The term neurodiversity was not recognized in Kentucky until 1999.

3.   (page 31) Autistic Behavior: in 1961, Autistic Behavior was described differently than it is now. Autism as we recognize it today was defined in the 1970s. Again, this is too complex a discussion for this forum.

4.   (page 60) Tuition at The Cove Schools residential was $500 per month, for 10 months, in 1963. Tuition at Harvard was $1,760 per year in 1963.(Source: Harvard Crimson November 17, 1964 https://www.thecrimson.com/ article/1964/11/17/columbia-ups-tuition-rate-another-200....)

Photographs

Unless otherwise indicated the photos used in this manuscript are family photographs that belong to or were taken by the author. Exceptions are indicated within the manuscript itself.

To Those Who Made This Memoir Possible

This memoir has literally been decades in the writing, so I am certain to leave people out who deserve acknowledgement. Still, it is important to try to begin the process of trying to be as complete as possible.

I begin by thanking my parents who did what must have once been unthinkable—send me to school 500 miles away from home and then continue doing so. I also must express my admiration for their not having divorced under the pressures of the moment: a child with exceptional special needs, a child whose needs were undoubtably shortchanges in the moment, a 'miscarriage' that resulted in a sister who only survived an hour: Sarah Inman McCann, a brother born prematurely—and that was only one year. There were undoubtably other stressful years; but 1959-1960 was undoubtably the worst.

I am grateful to my siblings, all four of them, who have grown to adulthood and have enriched my life.

I acknowledge the influence and love of my grandparents, uncles and aunts, cousins, roughly twenty on each side of the family. They supported my parents at what were no doubt among the lowest, darkest moments in their lives.

The Cove Schools and its marvelous and talented teachers and staff are people I will always be indebted to, particularly Dr. Marie Strauss. Dr. Laura Lehtinen Rogan whom my parents each acknowledged as having provided them with the knowledge and skills they needed to help me successfully transition to public schools here in Kentucky.

I also need to acknowledge my professors at EKU where I earned my MFA, especially Dr. Lisa Bosley and my thesis advisor Dr. Young Smith.

Writing this memoir was tremendously helped by individuals in Racine, Wisconsin, particularly: the staff of the local history room of the Racine Public Library; Lynn Biese-Carroll, executive director of the DeKoven Center and the Center's archival staff.

Today The Cove School is located in Northbrook, IL. Its Executive Director, Dr. Sally Sover, not only encouraged me to write this work, she also provided the many educational records upon which it is based. Finally, she wrote the Forward which will help put my story into a larger context.

Last but not least, never least, a huge thank you to my wife, Jeanine Grant Lister, who has encouraged this effort, helped with the research on our several trips to Racine, and Milwaukee, WI, and to Northbrook, IL, and for proofreading the galleys of this book as well.

My time at The Cove Schools, Racine, Wisconsin changed my life. Indeed it never would have turned out as it did were it not for my attending that school, and being exposed to those teachers and teaching methods. I am grateful to my fellow students who encouraged me and dreamed with me about the future that came to be for me, and I hope for them.

Yet I must also acknowledge that the life I have now is due to the visions of Dr. Alfred A. Strauss and the talents of Dr. Marie Strauss, Dr. Laura Lehtinen Rogan, Dr. Charles H. Bartlett, Edith De Moulpied, Herbert J. Olson, Laurel Schwager and the staff that made The Cove School not just a school, but a home.

William H. McCann, Jr.

Cyberwit.net
HIG 45 Kaushambi Kunj, Kalindipuram
Allahabad - 211011 (U.P.) India
http://www.cyberwit.net
Tel: +(91) 9415091004
E-mail: info@cyberwit.net

Printed at Repro India.